I0568055

MAKE WORLDS

Fear Is The Root of All Weakness®

ii

Anything but Ordinary

Judgement and Perception have NO value here. ©

AUTOBIOGRAPHICAL SERIES

© 2021 - 2026 **Barbwire Noose** | Australia
www.barbwirenoose.com | Marcia Anita Hobbs (BNoose)

Marcia Anita Hobbs (BNoose) | www.marciabnoose.com

Copyright © Marcia BNoose 2021/2026

Copyright © Marcia Anita Hobbs 2021/2026

This work depicts actual events in the author's life as truthfully as recollection permits.

This is a work of nonfiction. No names have been changed, no characters invented, no events fabricated.

The right of Marcia Anita Hobbs (BNoose) to be identified as the author of this work has been asserted by the author in accordance with the COPYRIGHT ACT 1968 – SECT 35, Ownership of copyright in original works (AUS).

All rights reserved. No part of this publication may be reproduced, stored in a retrieval system, or transmitted in any form or by any means, electronic, mechanical, photocopying, recording, or otherwise, without the prior permission of the author and/or publishers.

Any person who commits any unauthorised act in relation to this publication may be liable to criminal prosecution and civil claims for damages.

Anything but Ordinary - Judgement and Perception have NO value here series.

A CIP catalogue record for this title is available from the National Library of Australia.

ISBN 9780645786033 (Paperback)

ISBN 9780645786033 (ePub-e-book)

www.barbwirenoose.com | Barbwire Noose® Pty Ltd AUSTRALIA/USA/UK

Dedication

To everyone I love and to Justice for All. For everyone who believes in the Universal Declaration of Human Rights, shall Good always prevail over evil. A Better World. To Justice for All. Truth Matters.

Acknowledgment

To the Truth upholders and whistle-blowers of the world - together
we make 'A Better World'.

This Series of Books.

Autobiographies, A Brand Dedicated To 'A Better World' – Human Rights. The Autobiographical Series 'Anything But Ordinary – Judgement And Perception Have No Value Here' is a collection of books full of candid facts, Experiences, Quotes, and open to Interpretation, depending on where the Reader's head is at – Judgment, Education, My Life, And Thoughts. Stories Of The Heart, Mind, and Soul, Consisting Of Personal Views, knowledge, and life experiences, as well as light-hearted, Comedic References, Poetry, World facts, and More.

Quoting A Letter To Professor Fatima Meer From The Book 'Conversations With Myself' By Nelson Mandela: "The Trouble, Of Course, Is That Most Successful Men Are Prone To Some Form Of Vanity. There Comes A Stage In Their Lives When They Consider It Permissible To Be Egotistic And To Brag To The Public At Large About Their Unique Achievements. What a Sweet Euphemism for Self-Praise the English Language Has Evolved! Autobiography, They Choose To Call It, Where The Shortcomings Of Others Are Frequently Exploited To Highlight The Praiseworthy Accomplishments Of The Author."

As a true crime writer and author of biographical literature, I Could Relate To Nelson Mandela's View of Autobiography. Although I Have Ensured That My Life's Evolution, in Its Imperfections and Perfections, has been Equally Shared, I cannot help but feel at Times That the Personal Nature of my autobiographies has truthfully and graphically shared the Shortcomings Of Others, Not Just My Own. Being Mindful Not To Brag Yet Proud Of My Achievements, This Euphemism Interpretation Is Bang On The Realities Of A Biographical Record. The Highs And The Lows Of Life, Often Shared Moments. When The Hunter Talks Of Killing The Lion, It Is The Hunter's Life That Is Glorified, Though The Lion Has Great Achievements Of Its Own Unshared, As A Hunter Only Knows His Own Life And The Lion's Role In It.

MARCIA BNOOSE

ANYTHING BUT ORDINARY – JUDGMENT AND PERCEPTION HAVE NO VALUE HERE.

BOOK NO 4

(of however many books in the series I would like)

Contents

CHAPTERS ABO BOOK 4

REVOLUTIONARY FASHION

Every Barbwire Noose item I wear is either gifted to opportunity stores or upcycled (if in good condition). Barbwire Noose in 2023 launched a discount initiative to recycle old brand garments via Fashion Studies (Collarts College) and encourage consumers to engage more consciously with sustainable fashion practices. It involves encouraging purchasers to 'Get Involved' in this action by rewarding them with a discount for returning quality Barbwire Noose purchases after wearing them.

QUANTUM PHYSICS

Quantum mechanics is the science that deals with the behaviour of matter and light on the atomic and subatomic scales. It attempts to describe and account for the properties of molecules and atoms, as well as their constituents—electrons, protons, neutrons, and other more esoteric particles, such as quarks and gluons. These properties include the interactions of the particles with one another and with electromagnetic radiation (i.e., light, X-rays, and gamma rays). – Britannica. Quantum physics is the study of matter and energy at the most fundamental level. It aims to uncover the properties and behaviours of nature's building blocks.

I believe we are an infinitely greater metaphysical immortality. I think that quantum physics can prove the theoretical phenomena of life and time as materialised forms of energy.

POWER vs PEOPLE

"People Power" is a political term denoting the populist driving force of any social movement that invokes the authority of grassroots opinion and willpower, usually in opposition to conventionally organised corporate or political forces.

PIECES OF ME

Things you may know or may not know about me.

HISTORY

"History repeats itself, first as tragedy, second as farce." Karl Marx; German philosopher and economist (DOB 5MAY1818 – 14MAR1883)

MUSIC

Without music, life would be a mistake.

POETRY

Poems by yours truly.

JUSTICE

"Certainty is not overruled by doubt".

TRUTH VS LIES

Be careful what lies you tell about me; some dick heads may be corrected in these books. Defamation is costly.

FREEMASONRY

"Hell is Truth seen too late." - Thomas Hobbes, Leviathan

OPINIONS AND RANDOM SH*T

Opinions are like assholes: everyone has one—these are mine. Plus, Anything but Ordinary random sh*t.

Chapter One
'Revolutionary Fashion'

Every Barbwire Noose item I wear is either gifted to opportunity stores or upcycled (if in good condition). Barbwire Noose in 2023 launched a discount initiative to recycle old brand garments via Fashion Studies (Collarts College) and encourage consumers to engage more consciously with sustainable fashion practices. It involves encouraging purchasers to 'Get Involved' in this action by rewarding them with a discount for returning quality Barbwire Noose purchases after wearing them.

If you haven't read 'The Story Behind the Brand BARBWIRE NOOSE' – my brand - you may not be fully aware of what it is all about.

The slogan 'Fear Is the Root of All Weakness' represents the 'fear' that holds us all back. Holds us to oppression, slavery, dictators, and what holds us back in life in general.

The words 'Barbwire Noose' stem from the music band *Soundgarden* and their song *'Pretty Noose'* – the song singing the line *"And I don't like what you got me hanging from"* relevant at the time I registered the brands trademarks as the SA Labor Government had put me on six months full-time paid leave to oppress my reporting against criminal negligence I witnessed in Sharley House, located on Sharley Avenue, Mt Gambier, South AUS.

The crimes that I reported, which were committed against these disabled persons, are horrific—neglect, sexual abuse and cognitive abuses. As a nineteen-year-old, it was hard to witness, causing me much emotional distress, which is what drove the government to put me on paid leave. Upon returning to work after applying to IP Australia for my trademarks, the reprisal for my reporting was to be placed in part-time employment, providing care in more able homes. Stopping me from reporting on behalf of the people of Sharley House altogether. Disabled peers with the ability of babies – noncognitive, retarded, unable to communicate – these victims could not speak, write or sign – they could not fight nor save their own lives. Intellectual Disability Services Council (1976 - 2006), known as IDSC, rebranded to Disability SA, and the reports were archived, leaving the abuse unaddressed and allowing it to continue.

Paedophile Mike Rann (Born 5JAN1953) was the Premier of South Australia at this time, leading the South Australian Labor Government, and Jay Weatherill (DOB3APR1964) was the disability minister who furthered his career into becoming Premier of South Australia, leading the South Australian Labor Government. Both men accused of paedophilia in the state of South Australia –

both men became Premier of South Australia, like the broadly known in Australia paedophile Premier Don Dunstan (MP Labor DOB21SEP1926 – 6FEB1999).

It took years for my trademarks to be approved via IP Australia. The government, fully aware that if the brand BARBWIRE NOOSE were ever to succeed, its cover-up would be exposed. During the Disability Royal Commission held across Australia from 2019 to 2023, this is precisely what happened. Despite the government, police forces involved in paedophilia and other community members engaged in paedophilia working extremely hard to tarnish, disrupt and ruin Barbwire Noose and me financially, the brand has succeeded, and the agenda to push me to the refuge of suicide has not prevailed.

Barbwire Noose® is a revolutionary fashion. Since the Human Rights movement, the brand has expanded into an established streetwear line and a high-fashion couture line. It has operated in the sustainable fashion space, offering organic material alternatives in streetwear since 2008. It has also influenced both the Humanitarian and Sustainability sectors of fashion, as evidenced by the establishment of the website, brands' debut literature, and activism and policy and ethics beyond this time.

Brand Barbwire Noose is more than a brand—more than clothes; wearing the label is a statement. An empowering movement, built from a struggle for change against government authority in the disabilities sector and beyond, to create positive change at a governance level. Empowering lessons of civil disobedience – 'Do NOT Conform' moments.

'The Story Behind the Brand BARBWIRE NOOSE': *To tell The Story Behind the Brand BARBWIRE NOOSE® is to paint a picture of what led me to such frustrated emotions that I developed a brand of empowerment and a brand name like Barbwire Noose®. The literature you read—hopefully, immersing yourself in it—aims to paint a picture of my life's experiences that tells The Story Behind the Brand. The label is an extension of myself, my life, my One Love. It represents many things: the trials and enduring atrocities of government-sector corruption, and a movement toward 'A Better World'. A movement driven by my passion for justice for clients in the disability sector, a subconscious fight for myself, and Justice for All. I am so passionately infuriated by the lack of human rights our voiceless and most vulnerable persons have in our society. This outspoken, unconventional, 'Do Not Conform' Human Rights Activism is the brand Barbwire Noose—empowerment for a 'A Better World' activism defending human rights.*

The Oxford dictionary defines revolutionary as: revolutionary /ˌrɛvəˈl(j)uːʃən(ə)ri/ adjective

1. involving or causing a complete or dramatic change. "a revolutionary new drug" (Similar: original, unconventional, innovative, ingenious)
2. engaged in or promoting political revolution.

3. "the revolutionary army" (Similar: rebellious, rebel); a person who advocates or engages in political revolution.

Barbwire Noose Blog:

Unveiling the Story Behind Barbwire Noose

Have you ever come across a brand that instantly captivates you? Like, it's not just about the clothes, but the story, the fight, the message behind it? That's precisely what happened when I discovered Barbwire Noose. This isn't your average fashion label. No way. It's a bold, raw, unapologetic shout-out to human rights and social justice. And yeah, it's unique clothing branding at its finest.

Let me take you on a ride through the story behind this brand. Buckle up. It's gritty. It's real. And it's precisely what the world needs right now.

The Power of Unique Clothing Branding: More Than Just Fabric

Clothing is powerful. It's a statement. A billboard for your beliefs. But most brands? They play it safe. They stick to trends, colours, and logos. Barbwire Noose? They flip the script. They utilise fashion as a tool for social change.

Think about it. When you wear something, you're telling the world who you are. What you stand for. Barbwire Noose taps into that. Their designs don't just look cool - they mean something. They challenge the status quo. They scream for justice.

This is a unique clothing branding that doesn't just want to sell you a shirt. It wants to move you. To inspire you to act. To be part of something bigger.

The Origins: Where Barbwire Noose Began and Why It Matters

Here's the thing - every brand has a backstory. But Barbwire Noose's story hits different. It was born from frustration. From anger at injustice. From a desire to create a platform where fashion meets activism.

The founders didn't want to just talk about change. They wanted to wear it. Literally. They crafted designs that reflect struggles, resilience, and hope. The name itself, Barbwire Noose, is a stark symbol. It's raw, uncomfortable, and impossible to ignore. It forces you to confront harsh realities.

But it's not just shock value. It's a call to action. To remember history. To fight for a better future.

This brand is a beacon for those who refuse to stay silent. It's a badge of honour for the socially conscious.

The Art of Storytelling Through Design

Every piece from Barbwire Noose tells a story. It's not just about aesthetics. It's about narrative. The designs are layered with meaning. Symbols that resonate deeply with those who understand the fight for human rights.

Take their signature pieces—they blend gritty textures with bold imagery. The barbwire motif? It's a metaphor for barriers, oppression, but also strength and defiance. The noose? A reminder of past atrocities and the ongoing fight against systemic violence.

Wearing these clothes means you're carrying a story—a message. You're part of a movement.

And here's the kicker - the brand doesn't shy away from controversy. They embrace it. Because real change is uncomfortable. It's messy. It's loud.

How Barbwire Noose Connects With Socially Conscious Consumers

Look, if you care about human rights, you want your choices to reflect that. You want your wardrobe to be more than just fabric and thread. Barbwire Noose gets that. They speak directly to people who want to wear their values on their sleeves—literally.

The brand builds community. It's not just about selling clothes. It's about creating a space where voices are heard, where activism meets style. Where every purchase supports a cause.

They're transparent about their mission. Ethical production.

Fair wages. Sustainable materials. No greenwashing here. Just real commitment.

And the impact? It's huge. Wearing a Barbwire Noose sparks conversations. It challenges people to think. To question. To act.

If you want to stand out and stand up, this brand is your go-to.

The Future of Fashion: Why Brands Like Barbwire Noose Matter

Fashion is evolving. Fast. People want more than just trends. They want meaning. Purpose. Impact. Barbwire Noose is leading that charge.

They're proving that unique clothing branding can be a force for good. That style and substance can coexist. Fashion can be a platform for change.

And here's the exciting part - this is just the beginning. The brand aims to grow globally and spread its message far and wide. To inspire a new generation of activists who wear their hearts on their chests.

If you want to be part of something bigger, check out Barbwire Noose, the brand. It's not just fashion. It's a movement.

Wear Your Values Loud and Proud

So, what's the takeaway? Clothes aren't just clothes anymore. Their statements. They're stories. They're tools for change.

Barbwire Noose isn't just selling apparel. They're selling a vision. A fight. A future where fashion and activism collide.

If you want to make a difference, start with what you wear. Choose brands that reflect your values. Brands that don't just talk the talk but walk the walk.

Barbwire Noose is that brand. Raw. Real. Relentless.

Ready to wear your values loud and proud? The choice is yours.

The fashion industry is vast – we all wear clothes. Its impact and influence should be more positive than negative. Fashion has not only been an excellent platform for me to be who I am— exuberant, unique, outspoken, and out there—but also for making positive change and connecting with people. Every day, people — because we are the people —change the world. On both a daily level and a governance level. What we invest our time and money in matters. The choices we make regarding the disposal of clothes have a significant impact on this world. It takes little effort to donate your unwanted wearable clothing to your local op shop. It is not hard to use worn-out clothing items as rags before disposing of them, saving you money on paper towels. It costs nothing to think and think about our planet in the actions we take each day. Thoughtfulness and kindness, thinking sustainably and acting accordingly, make a difference in a world saturated with products to use, consume, wear – things to discard, neglect and abuse. Be kind to our planet; be kind to one another. The most revolutionary act in this world is kindness. Never underestimate the power of compassion and love. The most powerful force on this earth is love. Love this earth, love your neighbours – be kind, be revolutionary.

Barbwire Noose Blog:

Exploring Ethical Fashion

Let's get real. Fashion isn't just about looking good. It's about what's behind the seams. The choices we make when buying clothes? They echo far beyond the shop floor. Ethical fashion is influencing the industry, and it's about time. Do you want to wear your values? Good. You should. But first, you've got to know what's really going on.

Fashion is a beast. It's fast, flashy, and often ruthless. But it can also be a force for good. I'm here to break it down for you. No fluff. Just the raw truth and what you can do about it.

The Power of Ethical Fashion Influence

Ethical fashion influence isn't just a buzzword. It's a movement. A revolution. It's about demanding transparency, fairness, and respect for people and the planet. When you choose ethical fashion, you're saying no to sweatshops, pollution, and exploitation. You're saying yes to fair wages, sustainable materials, and respect for workers.

Think about it. Every t-shirt, every pair of jeans, every jacket has a story. Who made it? Under what conditions? What impact did it have on the environment? Ethical fashion influence pushes brands to answer these questions honestly.

Here's what ethical fashion influence looks like in action:

- Fair wages and safe working conditions for garment workers.
- Sustainable fabrics like organic cotton, hemp, or recycled materials.
- Reduced carbon footprint through more innovative production and shipping.
- Transparency in supply chains so you know exactly where your clothes come from.

It's not just about looking good. It's about doing good. And that's powerful.

What does fashion have to do with human rights?

You might be wondering, what's the link between fashion and human rights? It's huge. The fashion industry is one of the largest employers worldwide, but it's also notorious for human rights abuses. Child labour, unsafe factories, unfair pay - these are not just stories from the past. They're happening right now.

That's why the connection between fashion and human rights is critical. When you support ethical brands, you're supporting human dignity. You're standing up against exploitation. You're demanding that workers get the respect and rights they deserve.

Take the Rana Plaza disaster in 2013 - a tragic factory collapse in Bangladesh that killed over 1,100 garment workers. It was a wake-up call. Since then, many brands have begun improving conditions, but there's still a long way to go.

Here's what you can do:

Research brands before you buy. Look for certifications like Fair Trade or SA8000.

Ask questions about where and how your clothes are made.

Support brands that are transparent and committed to human rights.

Your choices matter. They send a message loud and clear.

The Environmental Toll of Fast Fashion

Fast fashion is the enemy here. It's cheap, disposable, and devastating. The environmental cost? Massive. Think water pollution, toxic dyes, mountains of textile waste, and carbon emissions that rival the airline industry.

Here's a brutal fact: the average Australian throws away about 23 kilograms of clothing every year. That's a lot of landfill. And most of those clothes are made from synthetic fibres that don't break down.

Ethical fashion influence means slowing down and buying less. Choosing better and investing in quality pieces that last. It means brands taking responsibility for their environmental footprint.

Some brands are leading the way by:

- Using natural dyes and low-impact manufacturing.
- Creating circular fashion - clothes designed to be recycled or composted.
- Offering repair services to extend the life of garments.

You don't have to be perfect. Just start somewhere. Swap fast fashion for slow fashion. Your wardrobe—and the planet—will thank you.

How to Spot Truly Ethical Fashion Brands

It's easy to get fooled. Greenwashing is everywhere. Brands slap on buzzwords like "eco-friendly" or "sustainable" without substantiating them. So how do you spot the real deal?

Here's your checklist:

- **Transparency:** Does the brand share where and how its clothes are made?
- **Certifications:** Look for credible labels like Fair Trade, GOTS (Global Organic Textile Standard), or B Corp.
- **Material sourcing:** Are they using organic, recycled, or low-impact fabrics?
- **Worker welfare:** Do they ensure fair wages and safe working conditions?
- **Environmental initiatives:** Are they reducing waste, water use, and emissions?

Don't be shy. Ask brands directly. If they dodge your questions, that's a red flag.

Remember, ethical fashion influence grows when consumers demand accountability. Your voice is powerful.

Your Role in Changing the Fashion Game

You're not just a consumer. You're a changemaker. Every purchase is a vote for the kind of world you want to live in. Here's how you can make a difference right now:

- Buy less, choose well. Invest in timeless pieces that last.
- Support local and ethical brands. They're often more transparent and accountable.

- Care for your clothes. Repair, wash less, and recycle.
- Spread the word. Talk about ethical fashion with friends and family.
- Get involved. Join campaigns or support organisations fighting for workers' rights.

Fashion can be a powerful tool for social justice. It's not just about style - it's about values. And when you wear your values on your sleeve, you're part of something bigger.

The influence of ethical fashion isn't a trend. It's a necessity. The industry is changing, and you can be part of that change. So next time you shop, think beyond the price tag. Think about the people, the planet, and the future. Because fashion is more than fabric - it's a statement. Make yours count.

1. Pictured above is the circular supply chain, crafted for the 2023 "Fashion and Sustainability" studies by brand founder and author Marcia BNoose. A study at the Arts college 'Collarts', unfinalised at this time due to police defamation surrounding cover-ups, whistle-blowen by Human Rights Activism.

Chapter Two
'Quantum Physics'

Quantum mechanics is the science that deals with the behaviour of matter and light on the atomic and subatomic scales. It attempts to describe and account for the properties of molecules and atoms, as well as their constituents—electrons, protons, neutrons, and other more esoteric particles, such as quarks and gluons. These properties include the interactions of the particles with one another and with electromagnetic radiation (i.e., light, X-rays, and gamma rays). - Britannica.

Quantum physics is the study of matter and energy at the most fundamental level. It aims to uncover the properties and behaviours of nature's building blocks.

I believe we are an infinitely greater metaphysical immortality. I think that quantum physics can prove the theoretical phenomena of life and time as materialised forms of energy.

It is proposed that there are predominantly six fundamental principles of quantum mechanics: the principle of space and time, the Galilean principle of relativity, Hamilton's principle, the wave principle, the probability principle, and the principle of indestructibility and irreversibility of particles.

According to the principle of Galilean relativity, if Newton's laws are true in any reference frame, they are also true in any other frame moving at constant velocity with respect to the first one. Newton's laws of motion are valid only in a coordinate system at rest with respect to the "fixed" stars. Such a system is known as a Newtonian, or inertial, reference frame. The laws are also valid in any set of rigid axes moving with constant velocity and without rotation relative to the inertial frame; this principle is known as Newtonian or Galilean relativity. A coordinate system attached to Earth is not an inertial reference frame because Earth rotates and is subject to acceleration relative to the Sun. Although the solutions to most engineering problems can be obtained to a satisfactory degree of accuracy by assuming that an Earth-based reference frame is an inertial one, there are some applications in which the rotation of the Earth cannot be neglected; among these is the operation of a gyroscopic compass.

Hamilton's Principle, also known as the Principle of Least Action, is a cornerstone of classical mechanics that states that the actual path a physical system takes between two states is the one that minimises the difference between its kinetic and potential energies.

Another explanation is to delve into the conversation of mass-energy. The idea of energy as a real constituent of matter has, however, become too deeply rooted to be abandoned lightly, and most physicists find it helpful to continue treating electric and magnetic fields as more than mathematical constructions. Far from being empty, free space is viewed as a storehouse for energy, with E and B providing not only an inventory but expressions for its movements as represented by the momentum carried in the fields. Wherever E and B are both present, and not parallel, there is a flux of energy, amounting to E $\wedge$ B/μ0, crossing unit area and moving in a direction normal to the plane defined by E and B. This energy in motion confers momentum on the field, E $\wedge$ B/μ0c, per unit volume, as if there were mass associated with the field energy. Indeed, the English physicist J.J. Thomson showed in 1881 that the energy stored in the fields around a moving charged particle varies as the square of the velocity, as if there were extra mass carried with the electric field around the particle. Herein lie the seeds of the general mass–energy relationship developed by Einstein in his special theory of relativity; E = mc2 expresses the association of mass with every form of energy. Neither of the two separate conservation laws, that of energy and that of mass (the latter, particularly, the outcome of countless experiments involving chemical change), is in this view perfectly true. Still, together they constitute a single conservation law, which may be expressed in two equivalent ways—conservation of mass, if to the total energy E is ascribed mass E/c2, or conservation of energy, if to each mass m is ascribed energy mc2. The delicate measurements by Eötvös and later workers (see above) show that the gravitational forces acting on a body do not distinguish between different types of mass, whether intrinsic to fundamental particles or resulting from their kinetic and potential energies. For all its apparently artificial origins, then, this conservation law enshrines a profound truth about the material universe, one that has not yet been fully explored.

In wave motion, the Wave Principle, also known as the principle of superposition, states that when two or more waves overlap in space, the resulting disturbance is equal to the algebraic sum of the individual disturbances. This principle applies to various types of waves, including water, sound, and electromagnetic waves.

Because of the principle of superposition, the old saying that no two things can occupy the same space at the same time does not apply to waves. Indeed, an infinite number of waves can occupy the same space at the same time. Furthermore, they do this without affecting one another, so that each wave retains its own character independent of how many other waves are present at the same point and time. A radio or television antenna can receive the signal of any single frequency to which it is tuned, regardless of the existence of any others. Likewise, the sound waves of two people talking may cross each other, but the sound of each voice is unaffected by the waves' having been simultaneously at the same point.

Probability theory is a branch of mathematics concerned with the analysis of random phenomena. The outcome of a random event cannot be determined in advance, but it may be any of several possible outcomes. The actual outcome is considered to be determined by chance.

Indestructibility (incredibility of particles) Theory: Theorists have sought to determine what makes up matter since the time of the Greeks. At the beginning of the 19th century, the English scientist John Dalton proposed an atomic theory that became the foundation of modern chemistry. His theory contained five main propositions:

1. All matter is comprised of tiny, definite particles called atoms.

2. Atoms are indivisible and indestructible.

3. All atoms of a particular element share identical properties, including weight.

4. Atoms of different elements contain different masses.

5. Atoms of different elements combine in fixed whole-number ratios when forming compounds.

Most of this information was sourced from Britannica, so if you're interested in more quantum physics, I suggest you start there. The links will guide you in understanding the ideas and ideals proposed by theories, and, in turn, you will begin to comprehend the universe, time, your connection to it, and that all energy has an impact.

Each individual on this planet is special – truly dynamic in their energy and impact. Some of us are more acute – yes (more intellectual), some of us are older souls and that existence gives us knowledge we can tap into. That said, the concept of time travel, as depicted in the movie 'Back to the Future', is not scientifically viable. Our connection to our universe and the purposes it serves are real. Ancient history symbolism holds many of the keys to further understanding quantum physics and the principles it studies.

Whether you have a great understanding or are just a beginner, the future (and our past) lies within Quantum Physics.

Chapter Three
'People VS Power'

"People Power" is a political term denoting the populist driving force of any social movement that invokes the authority of grassroots opinion and willpower, usually in opposition to conventionally organised corporate or political forces.

'The world is a dangerous place, not because of those who do evil, but because of those who look on and do nothing.' - Albert Einstein.

We all know that People outnumber Power. Yet power is always mobile, while the People are not. This is where tyranny, dictatorships, and totalitarian agendas overcome democracy.

Democracy involves People, totalitarianism involves Power.

The People will always have numbers on their side, and if they remember that they need to be active every day in those numbers, then Power is overpowered.

One voice can spark a crowd against power; it is the crowd that has the power. One voice can be silenced in ignorance and oppression, the Mob cannot be silenced so easily. Alexei Navalny (DOB4JUN1976 – 16FEB2024) is a champion of the People and knew these facts too well. One man can be stopped, but the mob cannot. Quoting the man – The LEGEND; Alexei Navalny (DOB4JUN1976 – 16FEB2024): "If they would kill me, it changes nothing" - "It's not about me," he said. "It's about people whom I represent or [am] trying to represent."

Alexei Navalny (DOB4JUN1976 – 16FEB2024) said in the Daniel Rohr film. "Listen, I've got something undeniable to tell you. You're not allowed to give up. If they decide to kill me, it means that we are firm. We need to utilise this power, not to give up, to remember we are a huge power that these bad dudes are oppressing. We don't realise how strong we actually are. The only thing necessary for the triumph of evil is for good people to do nothing. So don't be inactive." There is nothing truer than these words.

I am Australia's most infamous whistleblower. Loved by a lot of my peers (as well as loathed by paedophiles, who riddle the Australian population at this time), yet hated by many men in government and many in the police force. Sex offenders, mainly, I'm not at all bothered that they hate me. That said, the destruction I have seen as a whistle-blower opposing elite creeps and politicians has shown me the power of oppression far too often. I know the use of character assassination and ignorance far too well.

Power is not always about taking you out, as Vladimir Putin (DOB7OCT1952) did to Alexei Navalny (DOB4JUN1976 – 16FEB2024). It is a mission to keep you down, to hold your energy back. Prolonging its profuse return, which those involved in esoteric teachings know well. The power of one's destiny is immense, in both the good and the evil of this earth. An honest and accountable leader is best suited to lead a country – this is true of any leadership. Yet it is rare that the brave and sincere, the few, make it into power, leading a nation and working for the people.

The story of Nelson Mandela (born July 18, 1918, Mvezo, South Africa—died December 5, 2013, Johannesburg) is a prime example of 'People Power'. *'A Black nationalist and the first Black president of South Africa (1994–99). His negotiations in the early 1990s with the South African President. F.W. de Klerk helped end the country's apartheid system of racial segregation and ushered in a peaceful transition to majority rule. Mandela and de Klerk were jointly awarded the Nobel Peace Prize in 1993 for their efforts.*

Early life and work:

Nelson Mandela was the son of Chief Henry Mandela of the Madiba clan, a Xhosa-speaking Tembu people. After his father's death, young Nelson was raised by Jongintaba, the regent of the Tembu. Nelson renounced his claim to the chieftainship to become a lawyer. He attended the South African Native College (later the University of Fort Hare). He studied law at the University of the Witwatersrand, where he later passed the qualification exam to become a lawyer. In 1944, he joined the African National Congress

(ANC), a Black liberation movement, and became a leader of its Youth League. That same year, he met and married Evelyn Ntoko Mase. Mandela subsequently held other ANC leadership positions, through which he helped revitalise the organisation and oppose the apartheid policies of the ruling National Party.

From 1964 to 1982, Mandela was incarcerated on Robben Island Prison, located off the coast of Cape Town. He was subsequently kept at the maximum-security Pollsmoor Prison until 1988, when, after being treated for tuberculosis, he was transferred to Victor Verster Prison near Paarl. The South African government periodically made conditional offers of freedom to Mandela, most notably in 1976, on the condition that he recognise the newly independent—and highly controversial—status of the Transkei Bantustan and agree to reside there. An offer made in 1985 required that he renounce the use of violence. Mandela refused both offers, the second on the premise that only free men could engage in such negotiations, and as a prisoner, he was not a free man.

Throughout his incarceration, Mandela retained broad support among South Africa's Black population, and his imprisonment became a cause célèbre among the international community that condemned apartheid. As South Africa's political situation deteriorated after 1983, particularly after 1988, he was engaged by the President's ministers. P.W. Botha's government in exploratory negotiations; he met with Botha's successor, de Klerk, *in December 1989.'*

Adversity does not hold back a great leader. It makes a great leader. Alexei Navalny (DOB: 4 Jun 1976 – 16 Feb 2024) would have been an Iconic leader of Russia. Vladimir Putin (DOB7OCT1952) is a dictator who feared this—fearing Alexei Navalny (DOB4JUN1976 – 16FEB2024), yet Alexei Navalny never feared Vladimir Putin (DOB7OCT1952). He lived with pride and conviction and died with the love and respect of his people. Vladimir Putin (DOB 7 OCT 1952) will not die with the same respect and dedication given to his opposition. Although Alexei Navalny (DOB 4 June 1976 – 16 February 2024) never reached power, in history (in his next life), his energy is expected to have a greater impact on the world, not only in his own country, Russia, but around the Globe.

In 2025, I studied subjects of 'Graduate Certificate in Policy and Governance' at Queensland University of Technology online. To begin with, my marks were strong, and the teacher's support was not petty. As it was clear I had been a driving force behind the Royal Commission into Disability, legislative changes, and the authored book, support from those paid by the government wavered. That said, studies of policy often note that it does not necessarily solve problems and can even create them, underscoring that policy is a parliament-based form of governance and is not necessarily people-oriented, let alone in voters' interests. Even evidence-based policy (EBP) must contend with political pressure, media priorities, and electoral priorities to reach the policy table. From the study of the four subjects—justice institutions, policy, governance and justice; public sector research; and the critical policy skills capstone—I conclude that policy is not designed in the best interests of the people, nor is it subject to submission, subjectivity, or application. The red tape surrounding adequate policy review or cabinet submissions—such as the level of in-text citations, the required use of italics, and the reader's lack of need to view the data and research to make a judgment on the document—contributes to the fact that policy is often inadequate or non-existent. The process of policy officers' submissions is encumbered by petty bureaucratic requirements and few avenues for adequately and conclusively informing the politician, reduced to a mere recitation of facts used to persuade or dissuade an outcome.

The mark you leave behind matters, the energy you create, the time you dedicate to others – People Power will always outweigh Power. In people versus power, it is the one who gives up who loses. Never give up. There may not be a second chance in life at times, but every day, big or small, you always have the power to do good. The People, as long as they always fight for their control, have – The Power.

Chapter Four
'Pieces of Me'

Things you may know or may not know about me.

I am a firm believer in the idea that we exist in the image of God, not necessarily 'God' as Christianity teaches us through Jesus, but in the God of the universe. The great architect of the universe, that which created us–energy, the big bang theory, atoms and molecules which make up all life.

My favourite meat is Lamb! I love lamb SO much and never say no to a good lamb roast.

Eggs are my go-to meal. A boiled egg or an egg microwaved with ginger and garlic (if available), seasoned with salt and pepper, is my go-to lazy meal.

I wear my German Shepard dog around my neck or wrist. Rossi is my best friend. I would have both my dogs, Kuta (a Kelpie, Cavalier King Charles Spaniel, and Jack Russell Terrier cross), around my neck, but my parents had my dog euthanised without my permission. Which I will never forgive them for. Both of my dogs (the first of my own) lived to a ripe old age of approximately fourteen, were well-loved, and I miss them very much.

I feel deeply connected to my grandparents, Joseph Stanley

Hobbs and Mavis Unger, both of whom were robbed from me in their passing.

In 2024, I met a legend in South Australia named Max, who knew my poppa, Joseph Stanley Hobbs (aka Stan). They were friends in Port Adelaide, South Australia. Max and I got along well from the get-go. It was very refreshing to hear his South Australian National Football League (SANFL) chimney painting stories (also known as the Westend Chimney), on which Max painted the SANFL's football colours for years. Lucky enough to allow his son to paint this iconic monument of South Australia, which held great significance over decades regarding the SANFL. My poppa 'Stan', as he was known, playing for Port Adelaide, is featured on the club's history board and in photos kept in Alberton, South Australia. The home of the Australian Football League (AFL) team Port Adelaide is a derivative of the SANFL team. Poppa debuted in the SANFL in 1947 and played 47 games. The conversations about football were grand. Unfortunately, our departure after a 'fake' friendship on the old man's behalf, playing on my love for my Poppa, ended nothing like the pleasantries of meeting someone with common ground; the false pretensions of Max, set on harvesting a million dollars for his run-down, barely visited pub, is another story told in these books.

Barbwire Noose

Figure 2 Max, Truro Pub, South Australia and a message from his ex-wife to cook at the Pub, Ros.

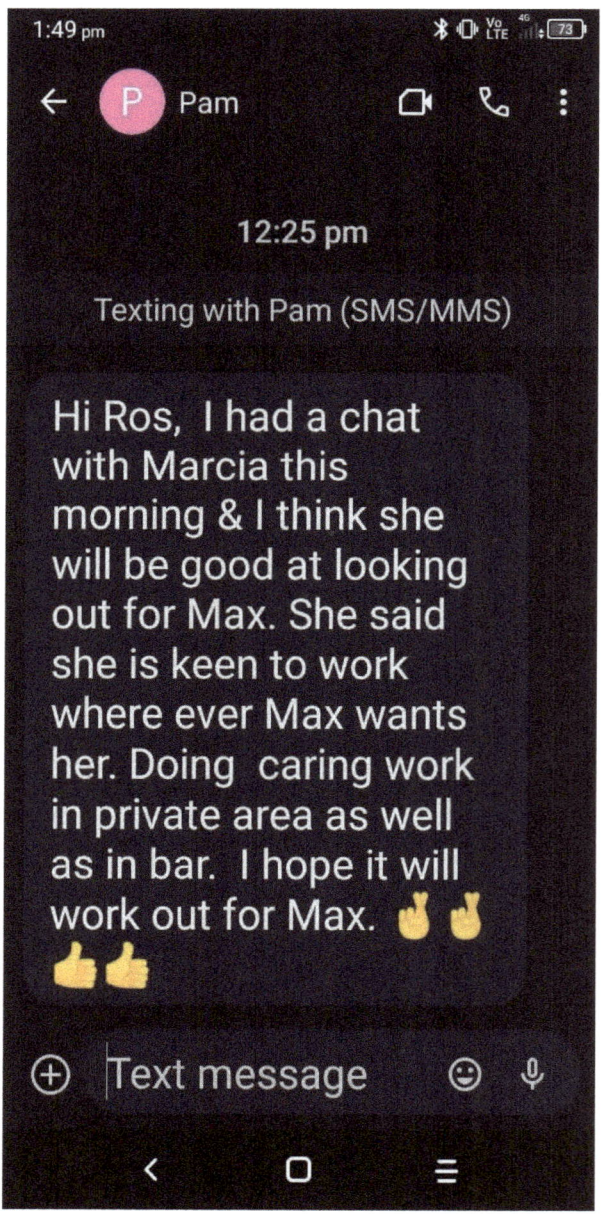

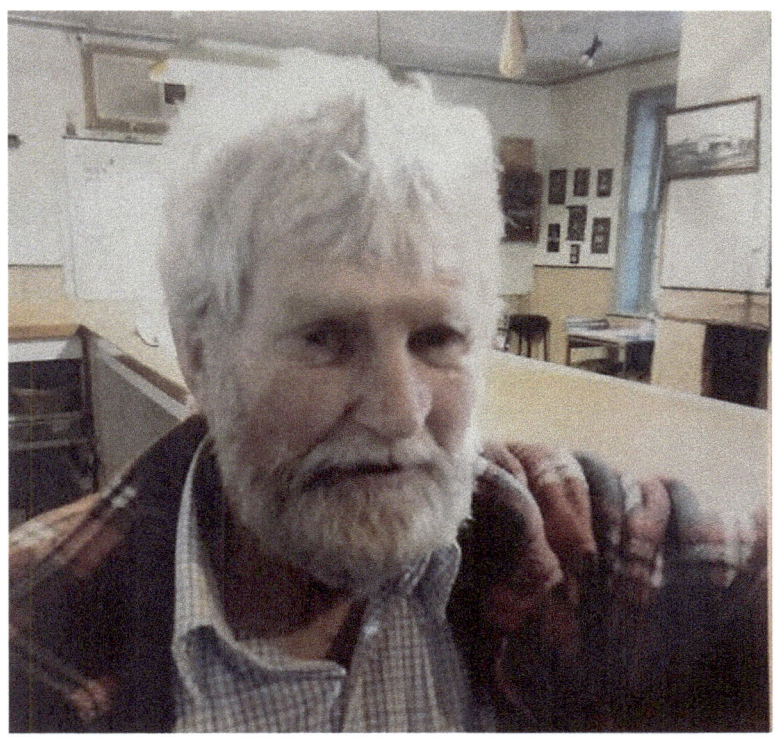

When I was a teenager, I used to illustrate horses. I had my own horse from around age 10 through my thirties, when my parents gave her away; I no longer rode her. She lived on my parents' farm, free, in the paddock. I was pretty good at drawing horses (if I do say so myself), yet when it came to drawing people, not so much. I tried numerous times to pull my brother, but I struggled to draw the face so that everything but the eyes looked good. The eyes not looking to flash made the picture evidently look drab.

My family (on my dad's side) has seafood at Christmas

every year. As my family are Port Adelaide locals, we enjoy the beautiful Semaphore Beach in South Australia. To this day, I still do not shell my own prawns, and if I am left to do it myself, even though I love prawns – my favourite seafood, it is highly likely they will go to waste. I'm not very good at shelling seafood, and the action literally puts me off eating them.

I am obsessed with shoes! I love shoes and can never have enough shoes. I mainly wear high heels, but I also love my boots and a few nice pairs of sneakers. 'Sketchers' is my favourite sneaker brand. My shoe size is small—five or six—and I can also buy children's shoes in sizes 13 or so.

My favourite perfume is 'Angel' by Mugler, described by the brand as an Angel Eau De Parfum spray, a tribute to the enigmatic and seductive power of femininity. The complex olfactory facets of Angel inspire confidence and grace.

Australia will always be home. No matter where I go, despite my Indian heritage background, no matter who I marry (if I actually say yes to anyone else other than Travis Paul Enmon Jr. (DOB: 16 Jan 1989), the great country of Australia is home to me.

I believe the eyes never lie; your soul pours out through your eyes and radiates your deepest energy—the window to your soul.

I have always aspired to live to be one hundred. God knows why because I hate ageing, have nightmares most nights and am completely traumatised by creeps, numerous cover-ups and Catholics.

I sincerely believe in ghosts. Hoping that my soul haunts all who have tormented it for the rest of time. That is my gift to those bad people upon dying.

Vitamin C, I think, is the most important vitamin to take. Its strength for your immune system and its properties that keep you and your body young are Amazing.

The greatest joys I have had in life have come from giving my time. Time spent with children (over fifteen years of aquatics teaching) and volunteering. Time to listen, time to help, time to give, care, walk, talk, stare at the moon, see new places, drive, listen to music, and be still. Time is the most precious thing in life. Cherish every moment.

There are a few television shows I will watch for life; no matter my age, I love Friends, The Nanny, Daria, Merlin, and Looney Tunes. I understand these are like mainly parental guidance shows – I don't care.

I am obsessed with gold and diamonds. This is what I waste my spare money on – jewellery, when I won representing myself against a significant police tort, acknowledged by the judge as institutional harassment in 2018 (- 2020). A case that my lawyer withdrew. I purchased a gold diamond channel ring, which I rarely take off. It is stacked under my two Tiffany & Co. rings. I will work with jewellery and shoes.

Django Hobbs, my pet Rabbit since 2024, is curious, clever, cute, courageous and quick. A black ball of fluff that is forever hungry and loves a gentle tickle behind the ear.

Once upon a time, I was taller than my brother – a long time ago, as pictured. I was like 8 years old. Bit of an exaggeration, but it was many moons ago, before we moved out of the family farm.

I've evolved from looking like my Mum to looking like my Dad.

I can't fish, not reliably well, at all.

Vitamin C is essential for me.

In 2025, I created a podcast called 'When Life Turns into a S**t Show. My opening video, which aired on YouTube, doesn't strictly fit the definition of a Podcast, but it featured Django, was quite funny, and was the most-viewed video on Barbwire Noose's YouTube channel this year.

I sleep in a bra – a bit personal; this Chapter is 'Pieces of Me'.

Anything but Ordinary

1. Me and my Bro with Shetland Pony 2. Me in October 2025
3. Podcast.   4. Life 2023 to 2024.
5. When Life Turns into a s**t show. 6. Django the Rabbito.

Chapter Five
'History'

"History repeats itself, first as tragedy, second as farce." Karl Marx; German philosopher and economist (DOB 5MAY1818 – 14MAR1883)

Donald John Trump (DOB14JUN1946) called for the construction of a border wall. Saying that, if elected, he would "build the wall and make Mexico pay for it". Donald John Trump (DOB14JUN1946) wanted to build a wall to stop the illegal immigrant invasion. The Mexico–United States border extends a whopping 3,145 kilometres (1,954 miles). To put that in perspective for Australians, it is approximately 3860 kilometres from Australia's most northerly point to its most southerly point in Tasmania. Can this be done, and will it work? Historical records indicate that the Great Wall of China played a crucial role in defending the Ming Empire against the Manchu invasions that began around 1600.

The Great Wall of China is a barrier fortification in northern China running west-to-east for 13,171 miles (21,196 km) from the Jiayuguan Pass (in the west) to the Hushan Mountains in Liaoning Province (in the east), ending at the Bohai Gulf. It crosses eleven provinces/municipalities (or ten, according to some authorities) and two autonomous regions (Inner Mongolia and Ningxia).

Construction of the wall began during the Qin Dynasty (221-206 BCE) under the First Emperor, Shi Huangdi (r. 221-210 BCE), and continued for hundreds of years across subsequent dynasties. The Great Wall in the present day is almost entirely the work of the Ming Dynasty (1368-1644 CE), which added distinctive watchtowers and expanded the wall's length and width. The now-famous national monument fell into decay after the Ming Dynasty, when the Qing Dynasty (1644-1912 CE) assumed power and expanded China's northern border, rendering the wall obsolete. Restoration and preservation efforts were only initiated in earnest in the 1980s CE, and the wall was designated a UNESCO World Heritage Site in 1987 CE.

The Original Great Wall of China:

During the time known as The Warring States Period (c. 481-221 BCE), the different regions of China fought for control of the country during the collapse of the Eastern Zhou Dynasty (771-256 BCE). One state emerged victorious from this struggle: Qin, pronounced 'chin' and giving China its name. The general who led Qin to victory was King Ying Zheng, who took the name `Qin Shi Huangdi' (First Emperor) after conquering the other states.

Shi Huangdi ordered the construction of the Great Wall to consolidate his empire and protect it against invasion. The seven warring states each had walls along their border for defence, which Shi Huangdi destroyed after he took power. As a sign that all of China was now one, the emperor decreed that a great wall would be built along the northern border to defend against the mounted warriors of the nomadic Xiongnu of Mongolia; there would be no more walls marking boundaries between separate states in China because there would no longer be any individual states.

His wall extended farther north than the present one, marking the then border between China and the Mongolian plains. The wall was constructed by unwilling conscripts and convicts who were sent north under guard from all over China for the purpose. Shi Huangdi was not a benevolent ruler; he was more interested in his own grandeur than in his people's well-being. His wall was not regarded by the Chinese people under the Qin Dynasty as a symbol of national pride or unity, but as a place where people were sent to labour for the emperor until they died.

The Ming Dynasty Wall (The Great Wall of China):

The present wall, whose image is so well known, is not Shi Huangdi's wall from c. 221 BCE. There is actually very little of the original wall left today. When the Qin Dynasty fell in 206 BCE, the country split into the civil war known as the Chu-Han Contention (206-202 BCE), fought between the generals Xiang-Yu of Chu (l. 232-202 BCE) and Liu-Bang of Han (l. c. 256-195 BCE). These two leaders had emerged as the most powerful of those who had helped topple the Qin Dynasty.

When Liu Bang defeated Xiang Yu at the Battle of Gaixia in 202 BCE, he became the First Emperor of the Han Dynasty (202 BCE-220 CE) and continued the construction of the wall as a means of defence. He was also the first emperor to use the wall as a means of regulating trade north along what would eventually become known as the Silk Routes (better known as The Silk Road), which the later Han Dynasty emperor Wu Ti (r. 141-87 BCE) expanded and opened for trade between China and Europe in 130 BCE.

The following dynasties made their own contributions and repairs to the wall until the Ming Dynasty initiated a massive building project to protect the country from invading nomads from Mongolia, the very same incentive that had informed Shi Huangdi's original vision. This similarity in purpose may explain the belief that the present wall dates from the Qin Dynasty. The Ming built the wall, featuring over 25,000 massive watchtowers, ranging in height from 16 to 26 feet (5-8 m), with a base diameter of 20 feet (6 m) and a top diameter of 16 feet (5 m).

The Liaoning Wall:

In addition to creating the massive wall, the Ming Dynasty also enclosed its most important agricultural centre, Liaoning Province, behind a walled fortification known as the Liaoning Wall (also referred to as the Liaodong Wall). This wall has been a source of controversy between China and North Korea since 2009 CE, when the Chinese government claimed it had only recently discovered portions of the Great Wall near the border with North Korea, in the Hushan Mountains.

UNESCO Archives.

Philosopher George Santayana originally wrote, "Those who cannot remember the past are condemned to repeat it". From this, we can derive that building walls to block out neighbouring people is not a solution to disputes.

Despite his divisive drive at times, you cannot take from Donald Trump's achievements his efforts and levels of persuasion and negotiation to bring peace, close to wars. A man of business and balls, he goes down in history as a leader of controversy, calamity, courage and cohesion. With or without his 'Big Beautiful Wall' between the USA and Mexico.

Chapter Six
'Music'

Without music, life would be a mistake.

This chapter is somewhat tongue-in-cheek; I hope my genuine love for music is evident.

Music is my go-to way of chilling. I feel like a broken record saying this. The band 'TOOL' is Epic – I have said this before. Jewel is my favourite moody-sounds, chill singer, and I often belt out the band 'Pearl Jam' on long road trips.

The word Music is defined as a noun: vocal, instrumental, or mechanical sounds having rhythm, melody, or harmony: the science or art of ordering tones or sounds in succession, in combination, and in temporal relationships to produce a composition having unity and continuity: a distinctive type or category of music.

My playlists are on Google Music, and I don't have Pandora, Shazam, or any of that shit. On my iPad, I have iTunes because I have to, really. Out of the hundreds of songs I have on my phone, I'm often listening to a few dozen, as most of us claim.

Live music is my favourite way of enjoying any music, and that's probably the only way you will convince me to sit down and listen to a country tune.

I have played a little bit of guitar, drums, piano and the recorder. I loved the recorder – no joke, 'Hot Cross Buns' all the way! If you don't know it, don't worry – I googled the lyrics for you:

Hot cross buns

Hot cross buns

One a penny

Two a penny

Hot cross buns

Give them to your daughters

Give them to your sons

One a penny

Two a penny

Hot cross buns

Hot cross buns

Hot cross buns

One a penny

Two a penny

Hot cross buns

Give them to your daughters

Give them to your sons

One a penny

Two a penny

Hot cross buns

These are sure hot

^ Hot as hey! Now that those lines are stuck in your head, let's talk about the song that never ends. It just goes 'round and 'round, my friends.

Some people started singing it.

Not knowing what it was

And we continue singing it forever just because

This is the song that never ends

It just goes 'round and 'round, my friends

Some people started singing it

Not knowing what it was

And we continue singing it forever just because….

Released by puppeteer Shari Lewis titled Lamb Chop's Sing-Along, Play-Along, in a 1988 home video – you want to kill her right, too late, she's already dead! R.I.P. (Shari Lewis, born Phyllis

Naomi Hurwitz; January 17, 1933 – August 2, 1998), you legend!

Back to seriously discussing music— kind of. Bob Marley, what a legend. A Jamaican singer, the man who made reggae. Bob Marley was born on February 6, 1945, and sadly died of a melanoma in 1981 when he was only 36 years old. A tragic story that he attributed to a soccer injury, when a dark spot appeared under his toenail, Marley did not realise it was a melanoma, thinking the spot was from his love for the ball game.

The 27 Club, as it is known, has claimed several musicians. Many of these deaths are attributed to the notorious use of drugs that plagues the music industry. Creativity has its price; the use of drugs can be enlightening, confidence-building, and enhance creativity, yet for many, the use has ended the lives of some of our most excellent musicians early, such as Kurt Cobain (Nirvana), Amy Winehouse, Janis Joplin, Jim Morrison (The Doors), Jimi Hendrix, to name a few.

Slipknot are a nine-piece band I fell in love with listening to the album 'Iowa' in 2002. They have a distinctive sound, with Corey Taylor exhibiting a remarkable vocal range. The band rose to fame following the release of their eponymous debut album 'Iowa' in 1999. I've yet to attend Knotfest —honestly, stoked that there are still some metal bands I'm looking forward to seeing, and that this festival brings them together! I have seen both Slipknot and Stone

Sour, which was SiC! I have a Stonesour guitar pick from the bass player, which is pretty groovy.

From guitar picks to drumsticks, to the after-party at the Big Day Out, to growing up around pub gigs and live music stories, to boyfriends who have been musos, my life has always been complemented by noise and by looking into the future; this does not look like it will change much. Developing my own sounds as we speak and having a stash of poetry, this hobby could be a one-hit wonder one day! No guarantees, but the one thing guaranteed with my own music production is that you will hear it on the Runways, where Barbwire Noose is showcased. I am so excited to be creating music that supports and even represents my Human Rights brand!

Music is a vibe, a feel, muse, a movement, a human, a group of humans, love, hate, lust – the inspiration of good and evil, pleasant and sad emotions.

Creating album artwork, vibe artwork, and other music-oriented graphics is just as fun as the creative process of music. Taylor Swift comes to mind with her 'Life of a Show Girl' album being released, as this book was physically published, and boy, was it a physical display of beauty and talent. Can't say I love every Taylor Swift song, but I *Love* everything Tay Tay – that chick got the goods. I'll never be this talented in music, and I am relieved that I am not going to pursue her line of work as a career. It's a hard act to follow. In 2025, Taylor Swift topping Madonna as the top-selling female artist of all time. Those ladies can keep that title. I'll aim for a Nobel Prize and may be a one-hit wonder.

Music is different for everyone, yet there is something for everyone, and something universal about it that transcends borders and cultural and linguistic barriers, and it has for centuries.

We send music into space, sing lullabies to our children, cry and console ourselves with birds singing or Taylor Mosman screaming. Music is life, part of life and can save life. Get behind local gigs, support the everyday muso, and feel what life is like—be immersed in the sounds of living, not just the daily grind of survival.

Barbwire Noose

1. Music STANDBY 2. Me and Shure :) xo
3. EP Trials   4. Modelling Music.   5. Music Production
6. Billboard - Iron Maiden.

Marciia

Chapter Seven

'Poetry'

Poems by yours truly.

SUMMARY 2019

Pure Disposition.

Demise.

I see you now with hollow eyes.

It cries.

The nothingness lies in you and me.

No light.

Nothing now so bright as the nothingness of this plight.

Blind.

I find everything.

To find nothing.

In you.

The nothing you have given to me.

Leaving an empty, hollow, unfillable void of turmoil.

Broken.

Bruised.

Bemused by pain.

Abused.

A walking pillar of abuse.

With only financial reign.

Empty gain and fame.

Amused by the unspoken.

Baffled with clarity.

We rise to die.

Fall to live.

Without life.

Love.

But an empty word that hope gives us to survive bad times.

Lust is an atomic must from a blocked gland.

Solitude.

An lonely word of understand.

Time does not heal all wounds.

Not Everything can be forgiven.

Trauma plagues a soul.

Never to be ridden.

29 October 2019.

Marcia Anita Hobbs, 1984.

UNIVERSAL LAW

This delicate ascent and descent.

Like tonic,

A hypnotic combination of beauty and danger mystifying.

A feeling that crumbled the hard exterior of the soul.

Emotionally crippled and intellectually suicidal.

 The door opened,

That Gaze.

Core shaken,

A piece of that soul taken,

Filling those eyes.

Electrifying.

A space encompassing hate,

Capture a moment so light,

So Right.

In a world of empty, cold social morality,

There is this.

There is unimaginable, unbreakable love.

Universal attraction,

A collision of the truest form of what we don't see.

That which we only feel.

Barbwire Noose

So great,

So far,

So fast,

That our descent is so brief.

We dissolve,

To resolve,

Love is the most powerful force on Earth,

In a world where power is nothing of love,

There is us.

A momentous moment,

In a moment generating such sensation,

Such engagements.

Divine.

You and I are here,

Right now,

Right where we are supposed to be.

Despite all this,

There is bliss.

There is US.

Author: Yours Truly, Marcia.
29 September 2018

KNIGHTS

How sincerity is greed,

How lust turns to need.

How fallen stars always shine,

Divine.

Fallen; Rise,

Fallen.

The dew of dawn is all unspoken,

As upon it reveals all of us are Broken.

The sweet whispers of loneliness -broken~men-

30 December 2018,

Marcia Anita Hobbs.

'Write me a poem', he said.

'For you I would write an essay on how the clouds kiss the sky, and the sun and the moon dance forever in a deep and distant romance.' I replied.

The Depth Of Divine

Encrusted in this engulfment of superseding infidelity,

Lovers a light among a wave of immorality.

The call of vanity breaks,

Like the blackened sky after a storm,

Engulfing the glorious blue in the sky it hides,

Clouds gliding and sliding across the mirage of day to night.

A lovers fight unfolded by mother nature.

As you caress my breast,

The clouds and sky coddle in and out of comforting embrace.

It is when the night slides into day,

And the day slides into the night.

That we see two lovers dancing across the sky,

Occasionally they pass and engage in a spectacular light display.

Like you and I entwined in the night,

Anything but Ordinary

Your body on mine.

Mine on yours,

The sky lit up at the sun and moons crossing.

Like the bedroom that flickers our silhouettes expressions,

The colours of the extraordinary eclipse.

You and I,

Limbs entwined glimmer as the skins sensations ignite.

Mystical and forever,

The explosion of a thousand kisses all over your body.

This is how the clouds kiss the sky.

2nd February 2020,

Marcia Anita Hobbs.

Hell and Sunshine,

That's how you taste,

Tantalising. - My Travis xo

Dirty Secret.

Your my dirty little secret boy,

The way you wear your tie.

How those sweat pants sit,

That bulge on your left thigh.

Your my dirty little secret boy,

When we cuddle up at night.

The taste of every sweet nothing,

You bring me such delight.

Your my dirty little secret boy,

The icing on the cake.

You make my body tingle,

With every move you make.

Your my dirty little secret boy,

My man, my boy, my guy.

Let's stay like this forever,

Together like the stars and the sky.

The following are untitled poetic notions, for me, for you, for someone. Enjoy x

To all that we feel and don't see, see and don't say and say and don't mean.

The Peace in Love and the Greed in Lust. - The Lust Of Love.

That something in your eyes that I could Love for the rest of time.

50 Times I Cried,

For That One Time You Lied.

And in the absence of Fear, it is not only ourselves we find, but life and death themselves. 23/03/16

Do not try to tame the beast within me, for if you touch the beast, it will devour you.

Love the beast, and she will purr like a gleeful child, touch the beast, and he will become wild.

Always remember that the evil Wants You to dwell on your mistakes. – Marcia Anita Hobbs, Lodge 406.

Chapter Eight
'Justice'

"Certainty is not overruled by doubt".

Justice: noun: the maintenance or administration of what is, especially by the impartial adjustment of conflicting claims or the assignment of merited rewards or punishments.

A judge administers justice in the Australian Democracy; a judge of an appellate court or court of last resort (as a supreme court).

The constitution sets the guidelines and limits within which the Government can administer the law among the people. The administration of law by the establishment determines our rights, and in Australia, it is supposed to be in accordance with the constitution, the rules of law, and equity.

Australia was a founding member of the United Nations (UN) and played a prominent role in negotiating the UN Charter in 1945. Australia was also one of eight nations that helped draft the Universal Declaration of Human Rights.

So, why do Australian governments ignore this charter and their constitutional obligations to the people when administering the law in modern times?

Here's my take on this.

The Charter was established after World War II, when the Nazis were defended by predominantly the United States, Great Britain, the Soviet Union, France, Australia, and New Zealand. These countries are fighting Germany and Italy in Europe, the Mediterranean and North Africa, as well as against Japan in South-East Asia and other parts of the Pacific. A battle of Democracy VS Dictatorship, where Dictatorship lost – Thank God.

From here, Australia took in numerous people from the battlefield of Germany who survived, transported via America to Australia predominantly by the Red Cross organisation. Survivors of these times have shared their stories with me. The most informative stories I have heard about this war came from a survivor named Kathy, who recounted her experience from 2019 to 2020. She was around 94 years old and shared her story of survival as a Polish woman with boldness.

Kathy was taken to a Nazi camp to work at a young age, lucky not to be shot as a Polish woman. Her German Aunt had taken her in as a refugee from Poland, and she was taken from there to work the sugar cane fields under Nazi rule. Pushed in the back and yelled at to 'work' in German, the word is 'arbeiten'. Kathy told me the graphic tales of her survival many times – hard to forget the tragedy she relived daily in her head. As an avid student of history, especially the Nazi era, I was immersed in her words, her hospitality, our friendship, and her kind nature, despite all the adversities she endured, including family dysfunction.

Kathy expressed that the Red Cross took her and her Nazi soldier husband, who claimed to be a Polish soldier, as the war was lost to America. They were processed by the Americans and sent to Australia, Melbourne, Victoria, where a large German camp was established. German finances funded the camp; Kathy was given German currency to spend in Australia and a German pension. Both the German and British currencies were in use before the currency was fully converted to the Australian dollar we know today. Many people – especially the wealthy of this German camp were gifted Australian land. The people of the German camp built many of the train tracks around Victoria and South Australia, spanning as far as Murray Bridge, and although the country was populated by what were called Ten Pound Poms. Ten Pound Poms were British citizens who migrated to Australia and New Zealand after World War II. The Australian Government initiated the Assisted Passage Migration Scheme in 1945, and the New Zealand Government followed suit with a similar scheme in 1947.

The country of Australia, taking in British migrants at this time, was already heavily populated with Germans and Italians aligned with the Nazi regime. The city of Mount Gambier, South Australia, where I grew up, is heavily populated with Germans who claimed they were from Poland to avoid the Nazi label, and was gifted much land by the Australian government in this region.

Australia was established on British foundations. If you research the alignment of British Royalty with Germany, you find many Nazi sympathisers. Charles Edward (Leopold Charles Edward George Albert; 19 July 1884 – 6 March 1954) was a British prince until 1919, the last ruling duke of Saxe-Coburg and Gotha, a state of the German Empire, reigning from 30 July 1900 to 14 November 1918, and later a Nazi politician. The popular Netflix series 'The Crown', which I love! Featuring in its fifth season a small but telling scene when the royal family learned of Mohammed Al Fayed's renovation of the home of the Duke and Duchess of Windsor, which he calls "Villa Windsor." Robert Fellowes, Queen Elizabeth's private secretary, informs the Queen that Fayed has extended an invitation for her to visit. "It seems there are all manner of valuable possessions at Villa Windsor, which we feel it would be important for the Crown to have back." Among those possessions, Fellowes shares, is "material relating to his wartime stay in neutral Spain and Portugal, where he and the Duchess were frequently in the company of Nazis, who hoped to install him as a possible puppet king."

Men have led the Australian government for over half a century. I personally am not surprised by unconstitutional laws established with a totalitarian agenda. That said, we are in an era of transparency—the newly established National Anti-Corruption Commission (NACC) has a pathway to create transparency in government. Justice is on its way to restore the rights outlined in our Constitution and uphold constitutional law, provided that the NACC is not led or infiltrated by the dictatorial practices of the past, characterised by seedy misjudgments and judges who reflect this in our current justice system.

That's my take for now.

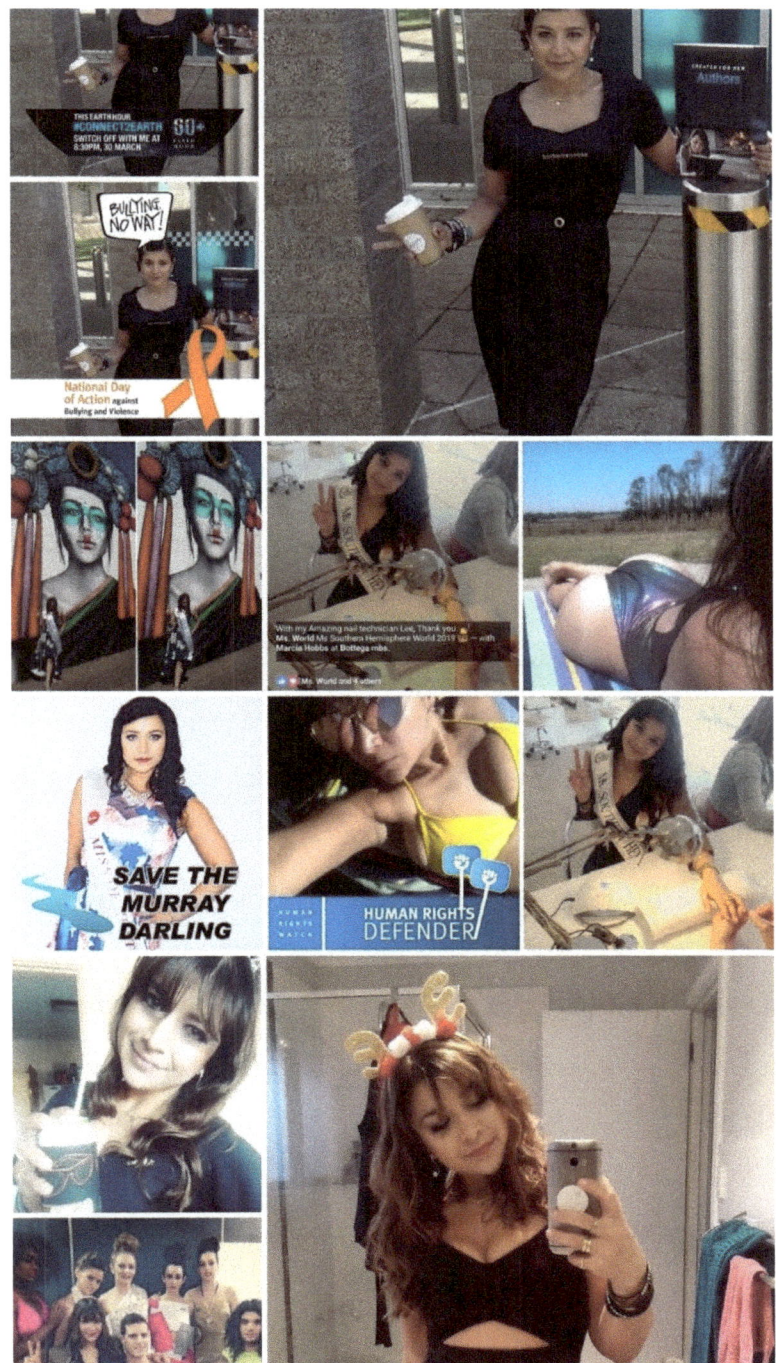

Chapter Nine
'Truth VS Lies'

Be careful what lies you tell about me; some dick heads may be corrected in these books. Defamation is costly. Perjury is a crime punishable by incarceration.

In 2024, it took a statement in a country pub for me to realise there was perjury surrounding my income and OnlyFans. I did not know police were trying to turn a platform I used against them, posting mainly images they had shared or imagery of less destruction than they had spread for ten years as a weapon. OnlyFans was not my primary source of income, and my bank account records confirm that. As an Australian citizen, the only way to withdraw funds from OnlyFans was to transfer them to my bank account. That stated, the proof is easy to put into court that this was police driven perjury to try and blame me for revenge porn circulated by law enforcement (Australian and International, naming the CIA) as well as organised crime for over a decade as if you do run a cover up of sex crimes, including children, disabled, and selling someone (numerous persons) on the dark web silk road. Yet, that is what the police did and hoped would get them through, using me as rape bait via STARForce SAPOL, to cover up criminal negligence and to negate the police status SAPOL issued without my knowledge or permission. The extraordinary emergency, reckless endangerment, and perjury I survived for over a decade after STARForce used me as rape bait for two decades is diabolical, and I personally think diabolical is an understatement. I quietly stepped off the OnlyFans platform in December 2025, feeling I had exhausted it as a basis for activism and action after approximately two active years, six months of this time when I was subject to incarceration torts without internet access.

The truth is, I have been single for a decade, spanning 2014 – 2024, after two life-threatening domestic violence relationships. I was forced into a relationship in 2018, which I did not allow to happen again, despite the efforts of two rapist. Numerous men claimed we were in a relationship simply because we spent time together over the past ten years. In 2024, I had a relationship with an American citizen named Eric, whom I should have left as a one-night stand; to be honest, it was more heartache than it was worth.

I was single throughout the entire year of 2019, raped twice by two persons known to SAPOL and STARForce. One of these rapists, before the sexual intercourse rape, tried to redeem himself as my friend by taking me on a trip he was going on at Easter. I reluctantly went on this trip because I was required to rent a room on his property, and he sold the house without securing another. Sold to a felon associated with SAPOL Hells Angels (HA) Graham Daniel Young, who is not really a HA. Staying in hotels before securing accommodation, paedophile and rapist Luke Ryan (DOB 1981, I believe) booked Riverview Rise Retreats as accommodation. I had suffered much sexual violence by this stage, and was used as rape bait by police forces. The trip was promised as a Rest and Recovery (R&R) trip for Easter 2019. After the property I was renting was sold, while SAPOL recklessly endangered my life, STARForce was trying to cover up over a decade of using my life. This trip was part of a further plot of perjury; Luke Ryan, a friend of my brother, Cheyne Michael Hobbs (DOB 9 MAY 1985), was involved in the perjury. At the same time, police forces across Australia plotted to try to make me homeless. Riverview Rise Retreats is located at 10182 Hunter Road, Mannum, SA 5238. The spa bath was disgusting. After I had filled and cleaned it, the accommodation installed a dirty filter in the system, which clogged it and caused the tub to fill with skin particles. The owner, at the time, claimed to be associated with the Australian Defence Force through their son and is guilty of perjury and violating health and safety regulations. The owner claimed that the paedophile rapist and I were on a date during my stay, saying that 'Luke Ryan' had claimed this, and the paedophile rapist claimed this trip was an Easter present for him after the fact. Not R&R, but an opportunity for me to utilise a beautiful backdrop to market my brand, as I do wherever I am. The incident, recorded in detail and in real time, is documented in the Autobiography UGLY HEROS.

Anything but Ordinary

The truth of the team of law enforcement who is most responsible for criminal negligence over my life before 2014. STARForce members are honestly the main team engaged in criminal negligence events surrounding me stemming from Kurt Slaven raping me in 2001 as a minor. Teams of STARForce members using me as rape bait over nearly two decades, the Australian Federal Police (AFP) in 2015 witnessed these out-of-control operations at times during the years 2014 to 2024, and are also guilty of severe criminal negligence in a sex crimes cover-up.

Peregrine Corporation employ many Catholics and is heavily associated with South AUS Hells Angels operations, sex offender Luke Ryan's brother, working as an accountant in association with activity negatively targeting me in 2019.

I owned five laptops in 2025. SAPOL allegedly possesses three of them. Plus, at least half a dozen phones, with SAPOL in possession of 2 (up to 5) for no valid reason.

In approximately 2004 or 2005, I wrote to the Dr Phil show expressing my concern for my dad's drinking. Dr Phil is an American talk show created by Oprah Winfrey and hosted by Phil McGraw. I love Oprah. I used to love the Dr Phil show, too. I no longer watch it, really. That said, they research and investigate stories for this show, both in the U.S. and internationally. The show never responded, but I love my dad so much I thought the show

75

would help him before there was an excuse to drown him with alcohol, either self-inflicted or maliciously.

I love taking a shower every day, but I don't wash my hair unless I have used hairspray.

I have not been a coffee drinker for my entire life, but I started in 2017. I have never been a cappuccino drinker and don't usually order such drinks in cafes. My history with cafes consists of ordering Green Tea, Mocha, or Chai Latte (half-strength if it's a Dirty Chai).

I have worked for an employer every year of my life since high school, except during the five years I have authored books, when I really worked my brand Barbwire Noose® and studied, except 2022 (end of 2021), where I attended the Alice Springs Casino, saving to take my brand Barbwire Noose® to attend New York Fashion Week. Over the past five years, I authored half a dozen books and earned numerous degrees, including diplomas and graduate certifications.

I like my boyfriend's fit, not fat. I have never had a boyfriend who was fat when we started our relationship, and never will. I believe the level of care you invest in yourself sets the standard for the care you provide to others. If you are too lazy to look after yourself, you will likely be too lazy to look after me, too.

I talk a lot, but I'm also thrilled to listen. If someone says I just talked to no end, and they didn't get a word in, that's bullshit. After a few hours, it is guaranteed that I would have grown tired of talking to you, at you, or to myself, so you'll definitely get a word in.

Am I a sexual deviate? I want to say this is none of your business, but apparently, it's been a topic of gossip for years. The short answer is yes, nothing weird or gross. I do not like old men, animals, or children. But I will have private fun, with probably fewer limits than most.

I do not like country music, nor do I like old-fashioned music, for that matter. The eighties have some cool ass tunes, but I'm a nineties kid with a passion for alternative metal.

Chapter Ten
'Freemasonry'

"A man cannot lay down the right of resisting them that assault him by force, to take away his life." - Thomas Hobbes, Leviathan.

In Freemasonry, an inquisitive mind is a necessary prerequisite. The pursuit of education is of the utmost importance. Not necessarily a formal education, but lifelong learning to better serve humanity.

Philosophy students are engaged in asking, answering, evaluating, and reasoning about the nature of reality.

Science is an education in the facts and methods of the Universe. A systematic endeavour that builds and organises knowledge in the form of testable explanations and predictions about natural phenomena.

The perfection of Humanity lies in compiling several invaluable esoteric, scientific, and philosophical educational resources and applying them to life.

Immortality, in philosophy and religion, is the indefinite continuation of the mental, spiritual, or physical existence of individual human beings. In many philosophical and religious traditions, immortality is conceived as the continued existence of an immaterial soul or mind beyond the death of the body.

Earlier anthropologists, such as Sir Edward Burnett Tylor and Sir James George Frazer, assembled convincing evidence that belief in a future life was widespread among peoples of primitive culture. Among most people, this belief has persisted over the centuries. But the nature of future existence has been conceived in very different ways. As Tylor showed, in the earliest known times, there was little, often no, ethical relation between conduct on earth and the life beyond. Morris Jastrow wrote of "the almost complete absence of all ethical considerations in connection with the dead" in ancient Babylonia and Assyria. (Source: Britannica, 2024).

At its core, Freemasonry is about the nature of truth.

Freemasons develop leadership skills in their search for truth.

Freemasons are supposed to strive for truth, both in their views of themselves and in their dealings with others. Masonry requires high moral standards, and its members and non-members should endeavour to uphold this principle in their public and private lives.

Freemasonry, in its broadest sense, is a system of morality and social ethics, a primitive religion and a philosophy of life incorporating a broad humanitarianism, without a creed, being of no sect but finding truth in all.

Honesty is of utmost importance in Freemasonry - "steadfast, trustworthy, and true," and "not to take bribes."

A music lover, here's a relevant music reference. Policy of Truth is the third single off Depeche Mode's seminal album, Violator. It was released on May 7, 1990. It reached number 15 on Billboard's US Hot 100 and number 1 on the US Alternative Airplay charts. The song is about living with the consequences of being untruthful. The song begins with the following lyrics:

You had something to hide.

Should have hidden it, shouldn't you?

Now you're not satisfied.

With what you're being put through

It's just time to pay the price

For not listening to advice

And deciding in your youth

On the policy of truth

It is a science which is engaged in the search of Divine Truth, and which employs symbolism as its method of instruction.

All Masonic teachings are based on truth, honesty, self-belief, and freedom from false influence.

In The Newly-Made Mason, H. L. Haywood refers to the obligations placed upon the new Mason: *"I hereby solemnly and sincerely promise and swear that as a beginning Craftsman in the Masonry of the mind and as a Newly-Made Mason I will not permit myself to be led into making hasty conclusions. I promise and swear that I will not listen to those who are not competent to teach me. There will be nothing binding on me except the truth. If there be those who say one thing and if there be others who say the opposite thing, I will consider that it is Freemasonry itself which finally is to decide between them."*

I, Marcia Anita Hobbs, am an unsworn Second-Degree Freemason, with knowledge in the Third degree extending to the thirty-third degree. The Second Degree, Fellow Craft, is the degree before the Master Mason - Third Degree. I have completed my Entered Apprentice First Degree and was set to be sworn (initiated) into the second degree before resigning in 2019 after witnessing Freemasons protect paedophile offenders.

I became an Entered Apprentice, having been Initiated on August 25, 2015, and resigned on August 15, 2019.

We are taught in the First Degree that the tenets of a Mason's profession are brotherly love, relief and truth. That the "Truth is a divine attribute, and the foundation of every virtue. To be good and true is the first lesson we are taught in Masonry. Yet I observed the opposite within my lodge and within law-enforcement Freemasonry. I am a Freemason by DNA, living on the square. I do not need a lodge to define my place as a freemason, as long as I am honest, moral and transparent when it matters and of matters. Regulating my conduct, influenced by the principle of truth, not hypocrisy and deceit. Sincerity and plain dealings distinguish a freemason. On 22 May 2024, I formally rejoined the lodge, clarifying that my membership was not based on my Freemasonry status but on the fact that Kurt Slaven was not an accepted Freemason. After a brief conversation on 22 May 2024, I initiated the process to rejoin.

Here are the communications thus far of that process:

Dear Marcia,

My apologies... the form you submitted said you were based in South Australia, and as Secretary, I was aware that you were not a current financial member, so I assumed you were an interested member of the public. I have now gone back to our records and see that you were an Entered Apprentice, having been Initiated on 25th August 2015, and that you resigned on 15th August 2019. Having resigned means that you are no longer a member and would need to re-join to become so.

I am a recent convert from the Male Craft to Le Droit

Humain and even more recent to the role of Secretary so am unaware of the matter you discuss but would say that within the male Craft Freemasonry of my prior experience there have been members with checkered pasts who have found redemption within that jurisdiction and are now men of strong and good character working hard to balance the scales as it were. All of us normally deserve second chances. That said, I respect an individual's right to decide what feels right and what doesn't regarding their membership.

Please let me know if you wish to rejoin and we will go through the usual processes according to the General Regulations.

Hearty good wishes,

SENDER: Steve Brown, Ill:.Bro - Wed, May 22, 2:51 PM (to Me)

'Unless your calling Kurt Slaven a freemason???

I refuse to rejoin then and you watch me bring this down on Freemasonry, not just police like Thomas Hobbes raging on UGLY lodge back in the day.' – SENDER: (me) May 22, 2024, 3:41 PM (to Steve).

Dear Marcia,

I have now had a chance to have a very quick look at some of the work you sent me and also to check through our records.

I can confirm that Slaven, Roche, and Kyriacou are not, and have never been, members of our Order. Not being aligned with the male Craft, I cannot speak to their status within that jurisdiction.

On matters that you raise...

The Middle Chamber was established by members of the male Craft, but was open to participation by members of the public, and on that basis, members of our Order did attend and present on occasion. Middle Chamber ended a few years ago. Our Order has established a similar forum that is open to the public called Societas Lux et Sapientia (SLS). It is 'open source' in that we do not curate the program—anyone can attend, anyone can present.

SLS is an open, informal group that meets to discuss a broad range of topics, including, but not limited to, those of a philosophical, educational, esoteric, and practical nature. Central to our activity is the promotion of free discussion and thinking through the provision of interesting and challenging speakers. The program is not curated other than the allocation of dates in the annual calendar.

While male Craft Freemasons attend and occasionally present, so do members of the public with no connection to Freemasonry of any kind. Presenters, however, are predominantly from our Order.

I attended and presented at Middle Chamber when a member of the male Craft, and that is how I found (and later joined)

Le Droit Humain. The Middle Chamber ended not long after I first saw it. In all my dealings with Freemasonry, I have never encountered the three men you speak of, either at Middle Chamber or at a male Craft lodge meeting. None of them has ever attended an SLS meeting.

Reading your chapter on Freemasonry and the reason you resigned from our Lodge, I can only say that my experience has always been a nurturing and positive one, and that the social activity (at the suppers, SLS, etc.) has been welcoming and friendly at all times. That said, the membership of the Lodge continually changes as new members enter and others leave, so I cannot comment on the composition of the Lodge between 2015, when you joined and 2019, when you resigned. The current membership spans a range of cultural backgrounds (English, Australian, Italian, Persian, Indian, Mexican, etc) and a broad range of beliefs from the very esoteric to the very rationalist, from the very progressive to the more conservative. With such a broad palette of views and members, it is hard to define our Lodge as having a dogma or single approach to anything, really. The ritual is the only consistent thread.

I am empathetic to what you have experienced, but I cannot, of course, say "I know exactly how you feel," as is so often blithely used in such circumstances. I hope that the legal matters that you mention are resolved as quickly as possible to enable you to free yourself of that burden.

Hearty good wishes,

SENDER: Steve Brown

Ill:.Bro Steve Brown 31o

www.freemasonryformenandwomen.org.au

Adelaide Lodge No. 406 - Secretary

Sovereign Chapter Rakoczy No. 72 - Most Wise Sovereign

Encampment of the Morning Star No. 160 - Grand Secretary

Adelaide Co-Masonic Assoc. Inc. - Secretary/Public Officer
Thurs, May 23, 10:32 AM

I understand it is a lot to digest.

I hope no one can truly understand the abhorrent experiences I have had. The legal matters with Royal Commission and AFP, they will certainly conclude.

As for the male craft, I understand UGLY acknowledged female freemasonry a few years back, so I'll kindly correct you that we are acknowledged by the male craft at this stage. Though some males like to keep their dealings with prostitutes away from their wives, the fact is broadly known and certainly not hidden at this time.

Lorraine Booth was part of my initiation. She is a 33rd-degree Mason, and her husband is involved with the Grand Lodge, which has seen her behaviour off-putting at times. Adrienne was excellent and is a great freemason of Co-Freemasonry.

The ideal direction for freemasonry is unity between the male and Co-Freemasonry craft during this century. Much respect for Freemasonry worldwide has been lost due to a boys' club mentality that protects seedy practices.

What is required to renew my membership, as I was scheduled to be initiated into the Fellow Craft and have the ritual notes prepared for this initiation?

SENDER: (me) May 23, 2024, 11:51 AM (to Steve).

NOTE: 23 MAY 2024 is a Full Moon in history. Mine, nor your spirit in good faith, shall be ignored. "So mote it be"

'At the heart of Freemasonry is the natural quest for Truth. Freemasonry is a means to self-realisation, universal-realisation, and for those so inclined, divine-realisation. Mysticism is the belief and practice that we can know the ALL through the inward way (reflection, contemplation, meditation, prayer, etc.). Whilst not all Freemasons are religious or spiritual in their practice, the system itself tends to encourage the pursuit of the ultimate Truth by turning our consciousness inwardly. More will be said of this in future degrees.' **- (Source: International Order of Freemasonry for Men and Women; LE DROIT HUMAIN Sydney Lodge No. 404).**

Extract: Thomas Hobbes, Leviathan - For the infallibility of his judgement concerning manners, he bringeth one text, which is that of John, 16. 13, "When the Spirit of truth is come, he will lead you into all truth": where, saith he, by all truth is meant, at least, all truth necessary to salvation.

Chapter Eleven
'Opinions and Random Shit'

Opinions are like assholes: everyone has one—these are mine. Plus, Anything but Ordinary random shit.

Always fill a hotel spa with hot water and soap before use. Run all the jets and drain the bath. The buildup of skin particles can cause illness. A severe lack of accommodation hygiene is illegal; paid accommodation must comply with health and safety regulations. Do not hesitate to complain if this is not the case.

Push-ups are a highly underrated exercise you can engage in anywhere, anytime.

Diamonds are a girl's best friend; well, they are my best friend. Be a good boyfriend and get your girlfriend a diamond.

I love butterflies and will literally walk with them if I can. They are so beautiful.

In my opinion, the legal drinking age in Australia should be twenty-one, and the blood alcohol limit in Australia should be .08% like in the United States.

I do not believe children should be voting in elections at sixteen years of age. Influenced by their family and peers instead of real facts, and outside of hormonal peer pressures. Leave the voting age to adults; if anything, raise it to twenty-one.

Home-schooling VS traditional schooling, well, I have friends who were homeschooled, and they are just as bright as conventional school goers. The only difference was their need to fit in, and the social interactions were awkward. I think if you are going to homeschool your child, you need to have them play sports and get out to socialise. Take holidays and interact with others.

Recently (2024), the SA Government announced that children should be 15 years old before using social media, and I absolutely agree. Children should not be burdened with adult issues, and they are overwhelmed enough at school with peer pressure and bullying. Get off the kids and let them be kids. Children must have a safe place at home to be, free from social pressure, school bullying and the bombardment of sex that plagues the internet. By 2025, Australia had enacted legislation requiring users to be 16 to use social media, with the laws taking effect in December 2025.

Some roads across Australia are so shit. The government needs to be held accountable for taking hard-earned tax dollars and squandering them on high salaries and wasteful practices. If you hit a pothole and it damages you or your car, sue. That will improve the roads, works in South Australia.

Studying with someone lazy or not on your level sucks, and

I think teachers should recognise this. As an acute and able student, I prefer to study alone. It really bothers me to hear people's excuses — "I'm too busy" —it might as well say, "I'm waiting for you to do all the work." Catering for our own busy lives is hard enough, then to battle with someone else's timetable too — especially when you're doing all the study work, it sucks.

Artificial Intelligence (AI) technology is currently out of control and unethical. It is a newly developing space that I believe governments are deliberately floundering in, overlooking policies and legislation to exploit new tech options for law enforcement and defence force systems, which leads to compromised societies and ill-directed political gains.

I think public transport costs should be capped, and those who are in poverty demographics should be able to travel on public transport basically for free.

Cash should NEVER be abolished.

Your body, your choice. Legislation should protect us in the future from compulsory bodily violations by the government or corporations. Get the fuck off us.

A controversial topic is animal testing. Rats and rabbits breed at an astronomical rate; however, this does not necessarily mean that animal testing is ethical – clearly, it is not. It is scientific and, like it or not, vegan or not, you benefit from science, and have for thousands of years. Who are you, really, to set the world back by saying that animals that are baited every day should not benefit the human race?

I think it is essential for workplaces to be diverse and inclusive, but I do not feel corporations should be incentivised to do this. The incentive scheme leaves people out and lowers not only workplace standards but also workplace morale, favouring government-funded diversity over the everyday hard worker.

In 2025, I received my third offer of admission to a university legal studies program in Australia and was enrolled immediately. Watch this space.

Everyone's shit stinks. Keep that in mind every day. You have at least one thing in common with someone you hate, and that is that you and they both have stinky shit.

Finishing with random sh*t from entrepreneur super mag BRAINZ Magazine October 2025 on me, the subject of the book – funny that: 'An Academic with a Diploma in Music and management, pending a Master's in Sustainable Fashion and a Master's in Business Administration and Legal Degree. Australia's Most Infamous Whistle-blower. Engaged in many Occupations: Acting, Modelling, Fashion Design, Authoring, Law, Politics, Government. Marcia Anita Hobbs carries the Princess title from her Indian Heritage. An Australian citizen born on Anzac Day, 25th of

April, in the year that challenged social and political themes, 1984. Marcia grew up to recognise the significance of both her birthday and the year of her birth. Princess Marcia, brought up in Regional South Australia, is no ordinary Princess. Known as the 'Rock Princess' of the pageant world due to her love of Heavy Metal Music. Marcia competed primarily in the pageant systems Earth and World, and debuted in United Nations pageants.

A self-proclaimed diva, Princess Marcia is a Freemason who left her initiating lodge after whistleblowing on the use of Freemasonry to disrupt and degrade persons in society. Marcia was brought up by professional parents who managed the Australian arm of Burger King Fast-food Family restaurants, Hungry Jack's, across South Australia.

The Princess, India Monarchy, British Indian Royalty, migration from India to Australia in the 1950s, Marcia's Indian Ancestry, hosting in Australia, the World-Famous "Curry Queen" Restaurant in Adelaide, South Australia, which for years catered to India's famous International Cricket team.

Marcia has held a National Police Clearance since age 16 and was accepted into Flinders University to study Justice and Society upon completing Year 12 in 2000. In 2021, Marcia was accepted to study for her Juris Doctor (JD) and Master of Laws at Flinders University in Adelaide, South Australia.

Marcia's Modelling background includes Photographic and Promotional Modelling. Her volunteering involves advocating for numerous like-minded organisations. Marcia volunteers as much as possible. Many efforts were directed toward causes aligned with the objectives of Barbwire Noose's 'A Better World' initiative. Marcia personally designed the Brand Barbwire Noose logo and registered it as a trademark with Intellectual Property Australia in 2005. Marcia is not only the Founder and Lead Designer; she also holds the copyright to Signature Prints and is a Signatory Designer for the Empowerment Collection 'Signature Puss'. The unstoppable entrepreneur personally handcrafts many pieces from the BN Couture and ACCESSORIZE collections—Pearls, Swarovski, Diamonds, and more.'

"I don't always do cool stuff, and I rarely think it's cool when I'm doing it. That's the beauty of life, if you give it a go, 90% of the time you will have fun! And that is cool."

Anything but Ordinary

Barbwire Noose

ONLINE INFORMATION

Socials:

https://www.youtube.com/@Barbwirenoose

https://au.linkedin.com/company/barbwire-noose

https://www.instagram.com/marciabnoose

https://www.instagram.com/barbwirenoose

https://www.facebook.com/BarbwireNoose/

https://mobile.twitter.com/marciabnoose/

https://mobile.twitter.com/barbwirenoose/

Websites:

https://www.marciabnoose.com/

https://www.barbwirenoose.com/

https://www.uglyheros.com.au/marcia-anita-hobbs

https://www.australianfreedomparty.com.au/

Other:

https://www.pageantplanet.com/profile/marcia-anita-hobbs

https://trove.nla.gov.au/search/advanced/category/books?creator=

marcia%20anita%20hobbs

https://issuu.com/lifestyle1-media/docs/lifestyle_1_issue_696

https://read.amazon.com.au/?ref_=dbs_p_ebk_r00_pbcb_rnvc00&_encoding=UTF8&asin=B08XJYTGLB

https://borderwatch.com.au/local-news/2018/01/06/lake-swim-lessons-begin/

https://borderwatch.com.au/features/2017/11/21/local-fashion-designer-takes-eco-fashion-week/

"Spring is Almost Over, So Step Into Summer Feeling Sexy and Swim Safe"

https://www.brainzmagazine.com/post/spring-is-almost-over-so-step-into-summer-feeling-sexy-and-swim-safe

"Secrets from the Eco Runway – Tips from a Sustainable Fashion Insider"

https://www.brainzmagazine.com/post/secrets-from-the-eco-runway-tips-from-a-sustainable-fashion-insider

"Barbwire Noose by Marcia Anita Hobbs Tells a Gripping True Story of Heroism"

https://www.brainzmagazine.com/post/barbwire-noose-by-marcia-anita-hobbs-tells-a-gripping-true-story-of-heroism

"Empowering Daily Boosts for Women in Leadership Who Are Ready to Rise Stronger"

https://www.brainzmagazine.com/post/empowering-daily-boosts-for-women-in-leadership-who-are-ready-to-rise-stronger

What if the judgments we carry are more about others' projections than our true selves? How often do you let perception cloud your uniqueness?

"Anything but Ordinary Book Series - Judgement and Perception Have No Value Here" introduces Marcia Anita Hobbs's autobiographical series, which challenges societal views of judgment and perception. She shares raw stories, reflections, and experiences that dismantle conventional standards and celebrate authenticity.

https://www.brainzmagazine.com/post/anything-but-ordinary-book-series-judgement-and-perception-have-no-value-here

Marcia Anita Hobbs, a fashion designer and author, is advancing human rights activism through her research-rich autobiographies, drawing on her experience as a former government employee, entrepreneur, and public figure. Political Prisoner 192703 is BNoose (Hobbs), the third international publication. Released via the National Library of Australia in March 2025, her highly anticipated third public disclosure autobiography is set for pre-sale in the coming months. Political Prisoner 192703, now available as an e-book PDF, with Olympia Publishers, publishing this gripping true story, which takes readers into a world of survival, resilience, and the will for the truth to prevail against life's devastating corruption and odds. The heartbreakingly heroic story of heroism in adversity, giving a whole new meaning to what 'Human Rights Matter' means in everyday, so-called democratic society. The book follows Marcia's real-time written experience navigating the chaotic justice system. With inspiring and hopeful quotes, this story of human strength will stay with readers long after they turn the last page.

https://www.brainzmagazine.com/post/political-prisoner-192703-by-marcia-bnoose-the-price-of-unlawful-enforcement

Anything But Ordinary – Judgment and Perception have NO value here.

BOOK No. 5

LIFE AS I KNOW IT

Forty-odd years of living life to the maximum I possibly could. This is what I know, what I have learned, and what I probably do not know too.

PSYCHOLOGICAL WARFARE

'Psychological warfare, the use of propaganda against an enemy, supported by such military, economic, or political measures as may be required. Such propaganda is generally intended to demoralise the enemy, to break his will to fight or resist, and sometimes to render him favourably disposed to one's position. Propaganda is also used to strengthen the resolve of allies or resistance fighters. The twisting of personality and the manipulation of beliefs in prisoners of war by brainwashing and related techniques can also be regarded as a form of psychological warfare.' – (Britannica, 2024).

ROTATIONS OF THE SUN

The Sun rotates on its axis once approximately every twenty-eight days. A female menstrual cycle is roughly the same. The Earth takes an average of three hundred and sixty-five days to rotate around the sun.

PIECES OF ME

Things you may know or may not know about me.

ROYALTY

"Civil society is a concept of peace between the peoples, authorities, and nations. Governments will elude any responsibility over a society they are ultimately allowed to flounder." – Marcia BNoose (Princess Marcia Anita HOBBS India/Australia), Le Droit Humain.

LAW

Legal Maxims Matter.

POETRY

Poems by yours truly.

THE FUNDAMENTALS OF LIFE

Meaningful origin, actions, and destinations.

TRUTH VS LIES

Be careful what lies you tell about me; some dick heads may be corrected in these books. Defamation is costly.

FREEMASONRY

"There is no such thing as perpetual tranquillity of mind while we live here, because life itself is but motion, and can never be without desire, nor without fear, no more than without sense." - Thomas Hobbes, Leviathan.

OPINIONS AND RANDOM SH*T

Opinions are like assholes: everyone has one—these are mine. Plus, Anything but Ordinary random sh*t.

EXTRA CHAPTER

'An extra Chapter, written in December 2025, because I can. From Margaret Atwood's "A word after a word after a word is power," to Ernest Hemingway's "There is nothing at all to writing. All you do is sit down at a typewriter and bleed," or Samuel Johnson's "The only end of writing is to enable readers better to enjoy life or better to endure it".

An individual is not subject to any civil, criminal, or Administrative liability for making a public interest disclosure. It is an offence to take a reprisal, or to threaten to take a reprisal against a person because of a public interest disclosure (including a proposed or a suspected public interest disclosure). The Federal Court or Federal

Circuit Court may make orders for civil remedies (including compensation, injunctions, and reinstatement of employment) If a reprisal is taken against a person because of a public interest disclosure (including a proposed or a suspected public interest disclosure).

It is an offence to disclose the identity of an individual who makes a public interest disclosure. Public Interest Disclosure Act 2013

No. 133, 2013 (Part 2; Subdivision A—Immunity from liability)

'Barbwire Noose', 'Fear Is The Root Of All Weakness', and the Barbwire logo are All
Registered Trademarks.

About The Author

Human Rights Activist Marcia BNoose.

Author, born as Marcia Anita Hobbs in Rose Park, Adelaide, South Australia, 25th April 1984.

In 2015, Le Droit Humain Co-Freemasonry, Lodge 406.

When the most Honest thing you can ever say is the Oddest thing you will ever say… "I wouldn't change a day or have it any other way." – Marcia Anita Hobbs, aka Marcia B. Noose, "Anything But Ordinary." – Judgment and Perception Have No Value Here; Autobiographical Series.

The content of this is Real. Candid, clumsy, courageous, and curious. Enjoy x

www.ingramcontent.com/pod-product-compliance
Lightning Source LLC
Chambersburg PA
CBHW051217120626
46547CB00013B/1391